**1.** Leveling up your craft to write a story that lives long after you've left the planet is what some might call a ridiculous goal.

**2.** You know that you will not tell that story after reading just one how-to-write book.

**3.** You know that you will not tell that story as the result of taking one seminar.

**4.** You know that creating a timeless work of art will require the dedication of a world-class athlete. You will be training your mind with as much ferocity and single-minded purpose as an Olympic gold medal hopeful. That kind of cognitive regimen excites you, but you just haven't found a convincing storytelling dojo to do that work.

**5.** The path to leveling up your creative craft is a dark and treacherous course. You've been at it a long time, and it often feels like you're wearing three-dimensional horse blinders. More times than you'd wish to admit, you're not sure if you are moving north or south or east or west. And the worst part? You can't see anyone else, anywhere going through what you're going through. You're all alone.

# WELCOME TO THE STORY GRID UNIVERSE
## HERE'S HOW WE CONTEND WITH THOSE TRUTHS

**1.** We believe we find meaning in the pursuit of creations that last longer than we do. This is *not* ridiculous. Seizing opportunities and overcoming obstacles as we stretch ourselves to reach for seemingly unreachable creations is transformational. We believe this pursuit is the most valuable and honorable way to spend our time here. Even if—especially if—we never reach our lofty creative goals.

**2.** Writing just one story isn't going to take us to the top. We're moving from point A to Point $A^{5000}$. We've got lots of mountains to climb, lots of rivers and oceans to cross, and many deep dark forests to traverse along the way. We need topographic guides, and if they're not available, we'll have to figure out how to write them ourselves.

**3.** We're drawn to seminars to consume the imparted wisdom of an icon in the arena, but we leave with something far more valuable than the curriculum. We get to meet the universe's other pilgrims and compare notes on the terrain.

**4.** The Story Grid Universe has a virtual dojo, a university in which to work out and get stronger—a place to stumble, correct mistakes, and stumble again, until the moves become automatic and mesmerizing to outside observers.

**5.** The Story Grid Universe has a performance space, a publishing house dedicated to leveling up the craft with clear boundaries of progress, and the ancillary reference resources to pack for each project mission. There is an infinite number of paths to where you want to be, with a story that works. Seeing how others have made it down their own yellow-brick roads to release their creations into the timeless creative cosmos will help keep you on the straight and narrow path.

All are welcome—the more, the merrier. But please abide by the golden rule:

*Put the work above all else, and trust the process.*

# CONVENTIONS AND OBLIGATORY MOMENTS

---

## THE MUST-HAVES TO MEET AUDIENCE EXPECTATIONS

KIMBERLY KESSLER

LESLIE WATTS

STORY GRID

# STORY GRID

Story Grid Publishing LLC
223 Egremont Plain Road
PMB 191
Egremont, MA 01230

First Story Grid Publishing Paperback Edition
August 2020

For Information about Special Discounts for Bulk
Purchases,
Please visit www.storygridpublishing.com

ISBN: 978-1-64501-026-5
Ebook: 978-1-64501-027-2

*For*

*All Past, Present, and Future Story Nerds*

## INTRODUCTION

The writer must know what genre they are working in and the conventions of that genre, just as a bridge builder must understand the science of foundational integrity and the means of mitigating stress on strung steel.

Why?

Because a story (whether it's a movie, a play, a novel, or a piece of nonfiction) is experienced by the reader on the level of the soul. And the soul has a universal structure of narrative receptors.

—Steven Pressfield,
*Nobody Wants to Read Your Sh\*t*

If you're reading this book, you have a story you want to share with others as a soul-to-soul connection, as Steven Pressfield would put it. The story comes from deep within you and is something only you can create because it comes from your unique knowledge and experience.

When your story first came to you, it probably started as an idea based on a setting, characters, or a problem. Maybe all three popped into your mind at once and you saw specific events unfolding like a movie. This initial spark and the ideas that follow are the raw materials of your individual expression. You know what all these raw materials mean because they come from your own imagination.

But in order for the reader's "narrative receptors" to connect with yours, you must include and arrange the components so others can recognize them as a story.

The good news is that storytellers have been constructing this kind of bridge for thousands of years, and they've left clues about how to do it in plain sight—within the stories themselves.

So, some of what you need to know to build your bridge has already passed into your storyteller's toolkit quite naturally as you've read books or watched films and television. For example, you probably know that a Master Detective Crime Story, like Agatha Christie's *Murder on the Orient Express*, must include a crime that is solved by a master detective who investigates the clues and evaluates suspects. You also know the story will kick off when a murder is discovered and end soon after the detective exposes the criminal and brings them to justice—or not. No teacher explained these must-haves to you. You know them because you've read books by Walter Mosley and Sara Paretsky and watched countless episodes of *Prime Suspect, Luther,* and *Law and Order.*

The specific details of each story vary, of course, but without the essential components or ingredients, a reader won't pick up the signal you're sending. Even if you nail basic story structure, unless you include the macro and micro components of your genre, the reader won't recognize it. If they open your book anticipating an exciting evening with a Master Detective, only to discover that the clues or suspects or—heaven forbid—the exposure of the criminal is missing, they will feel deeply unsatisfied. We've all experienced a story that doesn't work, and we know that's not what you want to create for your readers.

How can you avoid it?

You must build a bridge.

To conjure the overall experience of a

Crime Story, or any of the other eleven content genres we use to categorize stories, you build a bridge by employing the macro and micro components we call *conventions* and *obligatory moments*.

Now, it's important to note that conventions and obligatory moments are not cookie-cutter formulas that churn out cookie-cutter stories. The raw materials of your imagination are vital ingredients too. But in order to make that soul-to-soul connection with your reader, you have to look outside yourself to universal principles of Story, including conventions and obligatory moments. This will help you meet the minimum requirements to satisfy readers of your genre.

We're not going to lie to you. The distance between that initial cool idea you had and a story that readers of your genre will rave about is wide and deep. But you can break that distance into shorter spans by identifying specific tasks. When you can see each task clearly, you can craft solutions.

So grab your hard hat and put on your Story Grid safety goggles because we're going to show you around the bridge construction site. And to help you better understand the components, we'll use examples from stories you may already know like *Treasure Island,* a masterwork of the Action genre; *Murder on the*

*Orient Express*, a classic Master Detective Crime Story; and *Pride and Prejudice,* the quintessential Courtship Love Story.

By the end of this book, we hope you'll understand what makes conventions and obligatory moments so valuable and know how to use them to build your own bridges in the form of stories that touch readers' souls.

# 1

## STORY STRUCTURE

Conventions and obligatory moments are the components you use to create the bridge between the raw materials of your story and the mind of the reader. But they also link the structure and content of your story. Let's take a step back and consider what we know about Story and what makes it more than a series of interesting events. To get back to basics, we consult Story Grid's First Principles. (For a more complete review, check out *Story Grid 101: The Five First Principles of the Story Grid Methodology* by Shawn Coyne.)

What's the first thing we can say about the experience of any story that works? *A story that works is made up of large and small units.*

A global or macro unit is the story as a whole. An entire story combines structure and content to produce a specific experience for the reader. This happens through the structure and content of scenes, the building blocks of any story and the most important of the micro units.

To take a simple example we've already mentioned, the macro unit of *Murder on the Orient Express* involves detective Hercule Poirot investigating a murder to expose the criminal and bring them to justice. Within individual scenes, Poirot discovers the crime, gathers evidence, and interviews suspects.

What else can we say about stories that work? *Stories are about change*—both large and small.

We follow one or more characters on a journey to deal with external change in their lives *and* as they themselves change. The big-picture shift happens as the result of smaller moments of change within scenes that happen incrementally and in a particular sequence. For example, Poirot solves the murder because, in a series of scenes, he makes sense of the evidence and eventually creates a clear picture of what happened.

What type of change are we talking about? We're so glad you asked because the nature of the change is not a random thing. We'll get to that in the next chapter, but for now, we'll say the type of change is particular and the conditions for this change must exist within the story's environment.

Assuming you have the conditions for change in a story, how does it unfold?

Change happens when something within the environment upsets the current circumstances. Villainous pirates attack in *Treasure Island*. There's a murder on a train in *Murder on the Orient Express*. Two potential lovers meet in *Pride and Prejudice*.

Moments like these alter the life of the protagonist or their circumstances in some critical way, but the protagonist doesn't change fundamentally—at least not right away. After that kick-off event happens, the protagonist *wants something*, often to put things right, back to the way it was before, or as close as possible.

In our chosen stories, how does this desire manifest after the unsettling event?

- A person who witnesses an attack, such as Jim Hawkins, may want to escape or to find a way to dispatch the attacking villain.
- A master detective, such as Hercule Poirot, wants to find out whodunit.
- A potential romantic partner, such as Elizabeth Bennet, may want to get to know the other potential partner or get as far away as possible.

The protagonist translates their desire into *a goal* they can act on, and they pursue it.

- Jim Hawkins seeks help to escape the pirates and to save himself and others.
- Poirot secures and examines the available evidence to identify the killer.
- Elizabeth Bennet uses her wit to put Darcy off when she cannot avoid him.

While the protagonist may find support in the form of characters, circumstances, and events, they will also encounter obstacles that make things harder—usually much, much harder. This happens because antagonistic forces within the environment have goals that are in conflict with those of the protagonist.

- In *Treasure Island,* Jim Hawkins wants to save the innocent members of the crew, but he faces a group of violent and unpredictable pirates who want treasure and don't mind killing for it.
- In *Murder on the Orient Express,* Poirot begins to investigate, but the case isn't straightforward. Some of

the clues he discovers are legitimate while others are *red herrings* designed to lead him away from the truth. Understandably, killers don't want to be identified.

- In *Pride and Prejudice,* Elizabeth Bennet wants to marry for love, but other characters create obstacles for her because they have different goals. George Wickham wants to find a mate who can pay his debts and support him, Elizabeth's sister Lydia wants to have a jolly time, and Lady Catherine de Bourgh wants Darcy to marry her daughter.

In fact, conflicts *within* the protagonist may also get in the way of what they want. Jim doesn't immediately recognize that he, the country doctor, and squire are way out of their depth in attempting a salvage mission on a tropical island. Elizabeth can't see that her own prejudice stands in the way of accurately assessing how well-suited a mate is for her.

While the protagonist pursues the goal, they exhaust the straightforward options and their current skills fail them. They have tried to solve the problem (or take advantage of an opportunity) by relying on existing skills and know-how. And why not? Their old toolbox has served them well in the past. But a subconscious need, aggravated by their external circumstances, lurks within them. If they want to solve their external problem, they will have to give up what keeps them entrenched in old ways of seeing and behaving. That's because in stories, as in life, some of our old tools, designed for the challenges of the past, don't work so well when we face new ones.

Before they know it, an unexpected event happens that creates irreversible change but also helps them make sense of that earlier kick-off event. The need is no longer subconscious, and the protagonist faces a dilemma they can't escape. When the protagonist chooses an option, consequences follow as other characters and forces respond to their choice.

- After securing the ship from drunken pirates, Jim faces death as he falls into the hands of the pirates back on shore. He must decide whether to attempt escape or cooperate. Jim cooperates with the pirates and forms an alliance with Silver. Through this alliance, Jim stays alive and he and his friends outwit and defeat the other pirates.
- Poirot faces the possibility that the

murderer will go unexposed as he realizes the clues don't point to a single person on the train, and therefore, multiple people participated. He must decide whether to report all twelve killers to the local authorities or say the killer escaped. Concluding that justice has already been served, he decides not to turn them in.

- Darcy confronts his feelings of love for Elizabeth and proposes marriage, but when Elizabeth turns him down, he must decide whether to continue to pursue her or let her go. He lets her go, but when he has a chance to help Elizabeth, he takes it, and Elizabeth sees him in a new light and accepts his renewed proposal.

If this pattern of change we've just described sounds familiar, that's because it follows the Five Commandments of Storytelling, which you've probably studied in other contexts.

- The *Inciting Incident* is the event that kicks off the story by upsetting the status quo and causing the protagonist to pursue a goal.

- *Progressive Complications* are the escalating obstacles and tools the protagonist encounters as they pursue the goal, and the *Turning Point Progressive Complication* is an unexpected event that creates irreversible change and forces a dilemma.
- The *Crisis* is the dilemma the protagonist must face.
- The *Climax* is the decision and action the protagonist takes in response to the Crisis.
- The *Resolution* is the outcome of the protagonist's action, a response from other characters and the environment itself.

The structure of the Five Commandments of Storytelling forms the basic bridge that transforms the events of your story idea into a story. But we'll just bet you'd like a few more details about the bridge. Those details concern the nature of the change that happens in the story.

## 2

# GENRE CONTENT

Story Grid's First Principles point us to basic story structure with smaller sequential and incremental changes that follow the Five Commandments of Storytelling to produce the overall experience. This gives you a very basic bridge with anchorage points on either side and a deck that spans the gap. But the basic bridge is not satisfying to your reader.

In the same way that a story does not unfold randomly, the nature of the change that happens in a story is not random either. It is born of human needs like survival, connection, and R-E-S-P-E-C-T. These needs can be met or not in varying degrees, creating a spectrum of universal human value from negative to positive. Along the spectrum, we can pinpoint the state or condition of a person or character at any given moment in their lives.

For example, you can experience various

points on a spectrum from *hungry* to *full*. Before you eat, you're hungry, and after you eat a meal, you're full. More specifically, you can be a little hungry, "hangry," or on the verge of starvation. And you might eat enough to satisfy your hunger or overeat to the point of discomfort.

We could arrange these values in a logical order from those that are intensely positive (an abundance of nutritious food) to intensely negative (no food available or gluttony). This arrangement forms a spectrum on which we can plot the results of what happens over the course of a long period of time, in the macro, or a shorter period if we want to zero in on the micro. And really, that hunger spectrum is a very small part of the greater spectrum of values, Life–Death. The Life–Death spectrum represents our universal human need for Survival.

In *Murder on the Orient Express*, when Poirot discovers that Mr. Ratchett's death was murder, the value shifts to *Injustice*. Then the detective investigates the crime, which creates a small movement toward *Justice* on that spectrum. Within individual scenes, Poirot uncovers evidence that allows him to find the truth of what happened. He gets closer to or further from his goal with every piece of evidence he finds and makes sense of. By the end, we reach

*Poetic Justice*. The family and friends of Daisy Armstrong killed Ratchett because he was wrongly acquitted of the child's kidnapping and murder.

Each of the twelve Story Grid content genres aligns with a specific human need of the protagonist that determines the universal human values of the genre. Story Grid's Four Core Framework can help us see how four essential elements, starting with that specific human need and its corresponding spectrum of values, are at the beating heart of every story:

A basic *human need* determines the *universal human value* at stake in a *climactic event*, which elicits a critical *emotion* from readers. You'll find a full explanation in *The Four Core Framework* Story Grid beat by Shawn Coyne, but below are some brief definitions to guide you before we go over the specifics of each of our story examples.

- *Core Need*: The problem that arises for the protagonist at the beginning of the story is based on this need (survival or connection, for example).
- *Universal Human Values:* A spectrum of values (Death–Life or Hate–Love, for example) represents what

humans need to survive and thrive and reflects changes in the protagonist, who is acting to solve a problem and meet their core need.

- *Core Emotion:* The feeling (excitement or romance, for example) a reader experiences when the core value shifts decisively in the core event.
- *Core Event*: A story's climactic moment (the Luminary Agent at the Mercy of the Shadow Agent or Proof of Love scene, for example) when the core need is met (or not) and the core value attained. In this moment the reader experiences the height or depth of the core emotion.

Let's see how this works in the three stories we're studying:

- In *Treasure Island*, a global Action story, Jim Hawkins must confront violent pirates so he and his party can Survive (core need), causing a change from imminent Death to Life (core value) and evoking Excitement (core emotion) in the reader when Jim helps defeat the murderous pirates in the Luminary

Agent at the Mercy of the Shadow Agent scene (core event).

- In *Murder on the Orient Express,* a global Crime story, Poirot investigates the murder to achieve Safety (core need), causing a change from Injustice to Justice (core value) and evoking in readers a feeling of Intrigue (core emotion) when he shares his theory of the crime in the Exposure of the Criminal scene (core event).

- In *Pride and Prejudice,* a global Love story, Elizabeth and Darcy must learn to see each other as they truly are in order to attain Connection (core need), causing a change from Hate to Committed Love (core value) and evoking a feeling of Romance (core emotion) when Elizabeth learns of Darcy's Proof of Love and returns his affection (core event).

Each content genre's four core elements add dimension and detail to a basic story bridge, creating a specific experience. Crossing a suspension bridge is a very different experience than crossing a rope bridge—and each content genre leaves the reader with a different experience too.

When you know your genre's four core elements, you can begin to imagine the right *conflict*, *need, action,* and *change* in your story. The problem your protagonist faces is a result of *conflict* that arises from their specific setting and puts a basic *need* at stake. The protagonist takes *action* in pursuit of that need. The means to solve their problem must be present within the setting too. The means show up in objects and forces that respond to the protagonist's actions. The cycle of action and reaction causes a noticeable *change* in the universal human value, bringing the protagonist closer to or further from their need.

From here, it's just a hop, skip, and a jump to your genre's conventions and obligatory moments.

# 3

## CONVENTIONS

We often say conventions *set up* a story's changes while obligatory moments *pay off* the changes. We'll look at how that payoff works in a later chapter. For now, we just want you to understand that while the four core framework tells us what a story is about (core value) and even how it ends (core event), conventions create the potential for specific change and they are a vital component of the bridge you need to connect with readers.

So how do conventions establish the possibility for change that readers can easily recognize? They narrow a general problem related to human needs (How do we survive in an indifferent universe?) to a more precise problem (How do I outwit clever pirates trying to kill me?) by constraining the environment (e.g., a deserted tropical island in the eighteenth century). But conventions also give rise to possible solutions within the environment (e.g., a crafty threshold guardian who knows the lay of the land).

Our world is complex and confusing and dangerous at times—an interconnected web of causes and effects that are difficult to understand. Stories are elegant mental tools that contain and pass along solutions to problems we face as humans. Genre conventions help us focus and filter these problems and solutions through two categories of *constraints*.

*Selective constraints* are elements of the setting, or *arena*, that help define the problem in a story and put the core need at stake. We call them selective because they narrow the field of potential big-picture problems.

*Enabling constraints* are the characters—or *agents*—and circumstances—or *catalysts*—that make it possible to solve the problem. The setting or arena is there from the start, and enabling constraints arise as potential or actual instruments of conflict that force believable change along a spectrum of universal human values. In other words, they cause the effects readers expect to see in a particular genre.

Perhaps you're thinking that constraints will hinder your creativity. Maybe you're concerned your story will become formulaic and forgettable. In reality, conventions help rather than hinder because they're vital components of the bridge between your imagination and your reader. There's still plenty of room for individual expression, but you offer what's familiar (selective and enabling constraints) in a unique way based on your voice and experience.

Now, let's get familiar with the story arena.

## 4

## SELECTIVE CONSTRAINTS

The world you create in your story should send the message that a specific human need is, or soon will be, in serious jeopardy. Readers need to see and feel the conditions that create the risk. If you miss this step, their narrative receptors will cry foul.

Fiction, even though it's *fictional*, must ring true. We hope it's not too obvious to say the setting should include a location that *could* give rise to the kind of conflict featured in the story. You're looking for a context where the specific conflict is brewing just beneath the surface. The macro problem must make sense where it happens.

To find the arena that brings your characters' challenges to life, let your genre's core need and value be your guides. Imagine the kind of place where someone might struggle to survive, for example, or find love or gain freedom.

You've probably read or watched plenty of stories in which specific settings raise the expectation that trouble is coming. A claustrophobic labyrinth setting in a Horror story conceals life-threatening danger. In a Western story, the harsh, frontier landscape drives tension between an independent operator and the encroaching civilization. The vast canvas of multiple domains within a War story reveals what's at stake when a tribe or culture, not just an individual, must fight for survival. In a Performance story, a competitive arena generates pressure where characters risk shame when they attempt to live up to their potential.

Maybe it's less obvious in the setting of a Love or Morality story, but if you look closely the same principle applies. In a Love story, the setting begets *harmers* and *rivals* who try to keep the lovers from reaching connection and commitment. In a Morality story, the setting includes a seemingly impossible external conflict, such as a contentious divorce, where the protagonist must wrestle with their individual wants and the needs of others.

As you dream up the perfect location for your story's conflict, keep in mind that your story's setting has four main components.

## Location

Where does the story take place? Every setting has the potential for external and internal conflict, but the reach and characteristics of the location impact the scope of the problem. Traversing a more expansive landscape with multiple locations sets up a wide range of conflict as we see in *The Count of Monte Cristo* by Alexandre Dumas or in Robin Hobb's Farseer trilogy. A less varied setting tends to support multiple layers of similar conflicts. When we stay in one location, we can explore the internal landscape of the characters more extensively as in stories like *The Heart Is a Lonely Hunter* by Carson McCullers or *Bel Canto* by Ann Patchett. And then there are stories like *The Underground Railroad* by Colson Whitehead or *Death Comes for the Archbishop* by Willa Cather that give us the best of both worlds. The internal distance traveled mirrors the external journey.

## Period

When does your story take place? The time period, like the location, determines the capacity for conflict and the means of solving the story's main problem. The period imposes limits through available technology and prevailing social customs, among other things. If the story takes place in our earthly reality, the period would be either contemporary or historical. If it's happening in an alternate reality, it could be a hypothetical past, present, or future. *Brooklyn* by Colm Tóibín unfolds in a realistic past, the early 1950s. The events of the Harry Potter series by J.K. Rowling happen in a hypothetical contemporary fantasy period. *Leviathan Wakes*, the first book in a science-fiction series by James S.A. Corey, occurs in a hypothetical future when advanced technology called the Epstein Drive accommodates space travel throughout the solar system.

## Duration

How much time passes from the beginning to the end of story? This is not necessarily determined by the length of the story itself. *Ulysses* by James Joyce is a lengthy novel of more than 250,000 words whose events unfold over the course of just a day. But "A Rose for Emily," a short story by William Faulkner, spans decades in the life of a character. Because macro change happens incrementally over time in a story, the duration gives us a sense of the scope of the story's problem and how long it takes the protagonist to make sense of the inciting incident and solve the macro problem.

## Levels of Conflict

What types of potential conflict exist within the setting? Conflict drives your story and is an essential ingredient. Conflict arises when two forces act on their opposing goals or natures. We identify conflict on three levels: *inner conflict* (internal dilemma), *personal conflict* (between two or more people with opposing goals), and *extrapersonal conflict* (conflict between a person and the environment, including institutions). All three levels of conflict are bound to exist in any setting, but your setting should emphasize the levels that are most important to your story.

With all of these setting dimensions in mind, let's look at our primary examples.

The setting in an **Action Story** must always include the potential for life-or-death problems. In *Treasure Island*, author Robert Louis Stevenson uses three main locations: Jim's hometown on the coast of England near Bristol, the open sea aboard the *Hispaniola*, and a tropical Caribbean island.

Published in the late nineteenth century, the story opens in an unspecified year in the eighteenth century after the golden age of piracy. Billy Bones stays at the Admiral Benbow Inn for several months, and for several weeks Jim must wait for the journey to the island and back, which takes about five months.

Within the setting, a group of dangerous pirates with a crafty, shape-shifting leader want the map Jim possesses and the treasure it promises, and they're willing to kill Jim and others for it (personal conflict). The characters are susceptible to fatal tropical fevers circulating on the island (extrapersonal conflict). And Jim is unsure what strategy he should adopt to defeat the pirates (inner conflict). The three forms of conflict all impact Jim's ability to survive.

A **Crime Story** must take place in a location where injustice is a real possibility. Agatha Christie's *Murder on the Orient Express* is set on a luxury train traveling from Istanbul to Calais in the 1930s (a contemporary setting when it was published). From beginning to end, only a few days pass.

We feel the clock ticking because Poirot must discover the truth from a group of people with secrets they don't want to reveal (personal conflict) before they reach the next station. The characters are trapped because of a snowstorm (extrapersonal conflict).

The greater context of the story includes a justice system incapable of protecting law-abiding people and restoring justice (extrapersonal conflict). Before the events of the current story, Ratchett, who is really a notorious criminal called Cassetti, was wrongly acquitted of kidnapping and killing young Daisy Armstrong. Once Poirot susses the truth, he faces a dilemma about how to serve justice in this case (inner conflict).

A **Courtship Love Story's** setting must include obstacles designed to deny the lovers connection and commitment. The setting of *Pride and Prejudice* is Regency era England, a world of rigid class boundaries and strict standards of behavior. Most of the story events transpire in and around Meryton, a village in Hertfordshire. Some characters travel to London, Kent, and Lambton, a village in Cheshire near Darcy's estate, Pemberley.

The story unfolds over fifteen months, time enough for multiple inner conflicts to compound the lovers' personal conflict. Elizabeth and Darcy repent at leisure that they reached hasty initial conclusions about one another.

Elizabeth and her sisters face a problem common in this time and place. Most women couldn't earn an independent living, so marriage was the best way to achieve financial security. At least one of the Bennet sisters must marry a husband willing and able to support the rest, but the social rules of the time mean that the behavior of one sister could ruin the prospects of the others (extrapersonal conflict).

When author Helen Fielding designed her setting in *Bridget Jones's Diary*, a 1996 tribute to *Pride and Prejudice*, she had to adjust the protagonist's problem accordingly. In modern London, Bridget can earn money and live on her own. She doesn't need a partner. The conflict she faces is a more internal one—a comic exaggeration of her immaturity—that stands in the way of love and connection.

The setting of a story is more complicated than it seems at first because the arena must include all the qualities that make the problem not only possible, but imminent. Of course, stories wouldn't be very satisfying if the setting didn't also provide the means of solving the problem. For that, let's look at the second type of Convention—the enabling constraints.

## 5

## ENABLING CONSTRAINTS: CHARACTERS

As we've discussed, to build a story bridge, you must craft a specific setting using selective constraints where basic human needs are at stake and a problem is brewing just beneath the surface. But you must also introduce elements within the setting that enable the solution. Strangely enough, the solution comes through conflict because character change happens when they respond. *Characters* and *catalysts* are the source of this conflict and are your story's *enabling* constraints.

### Characters, Roles, and Agents

Characters are the individual human actors in a story, such as Long John Silver, Hercule Poirot, or Georgiana Darcy. Some stories include nonhuman characters too, such as Toto in *The Wonderful Wizard of Oz*, HAL 9000 in

*2001: A Space Odyssey*, or the bitter cold environment of the Yukon Territory in "To Build a Fire" by Jack London.

We say characters for simplicity, but when we refer to them in the context of enabling constraints, we really mean character *roles* because they fulfill functions and act as *agents* performing genre-specific missions. *Agents* are characters or entities that exercise their *agency* within their *arena*.

If that all sounds a bit complicated, fear not! We're going to lay it all out for you. Agency is simply the ability to respond to change by figuring out what's going on and deciding what to do about it. You do this every day, and your characters will in every scene.

Agents decide how to respond according to their basic approach to solving problems. In the Story Grid Universe, we've identified two basic approaches: *having mode* and *being mode*.

When characters embrace the having mode, they see the world as a *Power/Dominance Hierarchy*. They deal with change by trying to gain power and amass agency, often at the expense of others. Characters who embrace the being mode view the world according to a *Growth Hierarchy*. They focus on leveling up to secure the most agency for the most people. As you can imagine, these approaches oppose one another and create conflict, giving rise to unexpected events. (More on those in the next chapter.)

Let's say a person doesn't have enough food for their family. They can solve this problem in a lot of different ways. They might take food from someone else or find ways to improve food production. The first approach represents the having mode. If instead the hungry person seeks to improve the way they grow food or pools resources with others, they are pursuing a being mode approach.

Both approaches could be appropriate, depending on the circumstances. For example, in the Heinz dilemma, a person steals medicine they can't afford to save the life of a loved one. We may understand applying the having mode when it's a matter of survival but maybe not in the absence of life-or-death stakes.

As a story lover, you'll be familiar with many of the roles agents play. And chances are, you've already taken them into account as you've thought about who will inhabit your imaginary world. As you assign story missions, keep in mind that one character can perform the tasks of more than one role, and one role may be fulfilled by different characters in different scenes.

All of this is important because readers intuitively look for roles and agents. They are integral pieces of your bridge. If they aren't properly established, your reader will be disappointed. So what roles are needed in every story?

## *Luminary and Shadow Agents*

*Luminary agents*, typically called the protagonists, pursue the Growth hierarchy. S*hadow agents,* usually called the antagonists, embody an external force of opposition and pursue the Power/Dominance hierarchy. Even when the global conflict is internal—as in Status, Morality, and Worldview stories—a shadow agent generates personal or extrapersonal conflict that intensifies the luminary agent's inner dilemma.

In Action stories and Thrillers, the luminary agent is a hero, someone who sacrifices for the good of others. The luminary agent in a Crime story is most often a professional or amateur detective who wants to see justice served. In a Society story, the luminary agent is a representative of the underclass. But in a Love story, we simply talk about the lovers.

The desires of the shadow agent always stand in opposition to the desires of the luminary agent. In a Horror story the shadow agent is a monster that seeks to devour and annihilate.

Crime story shadow agents are criminals hoping to escape justice. Thrillers acquaint us with a master villain who needs the luminary agent to achieve what they want. The shadow agent in a Society story is a tyrant who deprives members of the underclass of their agency. In a Love story, there is usually a whole group of "harmers" who want to keep lovers apart.

### Other Character Roles

Luminary and shadow agents alone rarely provide enough conflict to satisfy your reader. Additional character roles are necessary. Let's look at a few examples from the Harry Potter series.

- *Mentors*, like Professor Dumbledore, have experience or knowledge in the arena and offer guidance to the luminary agent that can challenge their worldview.
- *Shapeshifters,* like Professor Snape, say one thing and do another to confuse the protagonist.
- *Sidekicks,* like Ron or Hermione, assist the luminary agent in their task but also generate additional conflict by getting in harm's way or

opposing the protagonist's decisions.

- *Threshold guardians*, like Hagrid, explain the way things are in an unfamiliar domain.
- *Tricksters,* like the Weasley twins, introduce chaos and point out hypocrisy.

Let's take a look at a few of the important character roles in our chosen novels.

In *Treasure Island*, Jim Hawkins is a luminary agent, but through most of the book he and the innocent crew members fulfill the agency-deprived role typically called *the victim*. The main villain or shadow agent is Long John Silver, who is also a charming shapeshifter and threshold guardian. Dr. Livesey serves as mentor to Jim, and Ben Gunn is a marooned sailor and threshold guardian.

In *Murder on the Orient Express*, Poirot uses his brilliant mind to follow clues and solve the crime, and he is the luminary agent. To some extent, almost all the other passengers on the train participate in the murder and cover-up, so they are antagonists and shapeshifters, but they pursue the Growth hierarchy, seeking to restore justice denied by Ratchett and a broken system, the primary shadow agents.

In *Pride and Prejudice,* Elizabeth and Darcy

are luminary agents and *lovers* with high standards. Lady Catherine de Bourgh is one shadow agent, a *harmer* who wants to keep the lovers apart. George Wickham is a classic shapeshifter and shadow agent. Georgiana Darcy and Elizabeth's aunt and uncle serve as *helpers*, bringing the lovers together.

Characters pursuing their desires and goals create conflict in the story, forcing the protagonist or luminary agent to change, but these actors need the support of catalysts to create life-altering discord in the arena. We'll take a look at them next.

## 6

## ENABLING CONSTRAINTS: CATALYSTS

As enabling constraints, catalysts move the plot forward. How do they do this? They operate on two basic levels to create conflict. From the outside, catalysts exert pressure on the luminary agent that mimics a kind of push and pull movement. They can't solve the external problem easily, and they can't simply quit and go home. This heightened *personal or extrapersonal conflict* requires the luminary agent to stay in the ring long enough to confront their *inner conflict* about the problem raised by the inciting incident.

Let's look at a couple of genre-specific examples.

### Horror

Horror stories have a unique catalyst in the nature of the shadow agent as *a monster that can't be reasoned with.* This makes sense because the monster is the luminary agent's worst fears manifest. Fear can't be reasoned with, and the monster won't give up under any circumstances. This catalyst magnifies other conflicts, complicating the luminary agent's pursuit of safety (core need). The pressure compels them to find the courage to face their fears. In the 2017 film *Get Out*, written and directed by Jordan Peele, the shadow agent is a monstrous white family that enslaves the minds of Black men, like luminary agent Chris Washington, so they can steal their bodies. When Washington finally makes sense of the awkward events in the house, he does what is necessary to escape.

## Society

In Society stories, *the vanquished are doomed to exile.* The shadow agent, or tyrant, understands this fundamental truth and therefore leverages all their resources and agency to crush rebellion and avoid exile. The relentless pressure compels the luminary agent to realize that recognition (core need) requires courage to expose the tyrant's lies, even as they risk other needs, like survival, safety, or connection. In *Ragtime* by E.L. Doctorow, authority figures who represent the state and individuals with a personal relationship with Coalhouse Walker urge him to give up his fight for recognition of the wrongs done to him to avoid prison or death. He chooses certain death to expose the hypocrisy of institutions and individuals and to save the lives of the young men who support him.

Now let's consider examples from our masterworks.

## Action

In an Action story, like *Treasure Island*, the *speech in praise of the shadow agent* establishes the large power divide between the shadow and luminary agents. We also learn the shadow agent's point, or what they want and why. The *luminary agent's object of desire* is to save the agency-deprived victim and defeat the shadow agent. That goal drives the protagonist forward despite the *power divide* between the two agents, which is also a catalyst. The conflicting goals mean both will fight to the very end.

Long John Silver delivers this speech while recruiting Dick, a young member of the crew. Jim learns that Silver wants the treasure for financial security and that the pirate risks hanging if caught by the British authorities, so he's planning to kill the honest members of the crew. Even among the fiercest pirates, Silver is feared because he is ruthless and cunning. Jim realizes that Silver's charm caused him to ignore the warning about a seafaring man with one leg.

## Crime

In a Crime story, like *Murder on the Orient Express*, a *ticking clock* forces the detective in a Crime story to eliminate *red herrings* and solve *the clues* quickly or risk injustice or worse. Poirot must sort through the conflicting clues to solve the crime before the train reaches the station, giving the murderer time to escape. Poirot discovers twelve stab wounds inflicted by different people, a red herring and clue meant to mislead investigators. By paying attention to human behavior, Poirot sees through the red herrings.

## Love

In a Love Story, like *Pride and Prejudice*, *Secrets* kept by and from the lovers generate conflict because they open a gap between what the characters want to do and what they feel they must do. Society keeps secrets from the couple, and the couple keep secrets from society and each other, but the biggest catalyst creating internal conflict is the secret each lover keeps from themselves. Love requires self-reflection and growth, so they must come to terms with their secrets. *Rituals*, though, bond the lovers to one another through shared experience.

Elizabeth doesn't tell Darcy when her feelings toward him change, and Darcy keeps his proof of love secret, even after they reconnect. They keep these secrets until they can each confront their own personal secrets. They must confront the truth about themselves if they are going to have any chance of commitment. Darcy must abandon his pride and attachment to his reputation; Elizabeth must let go of her prejudice against people within high society. Elizabeth and Darcy engage in witty banter and tease each other, which they don't do with any other characters. Whether they are loving or hating each other in the moment, they can always trade jibes.

Let's recap the mechanics of creating the conditions for change in your story through conventions:

- Conventions include the *selective constraints* of your global setting, which narrow the types of problems that are possible.
- Conventions also include *enabling*

*constraints,* the character roles and catalysts that give rise to conflicts and compel change.

- Together your story's Conventions create situations that reflect real life and cause believable conflict within the characters, leading them to act and react in new ways. These changes in behavior cause *universal human value changes* in the macro and micro units of your story, not the least of which are the obligatory moments that carry your reader across the bridge of your story for the payoff.

## 7

## OBLIGATORY MOMENTS

Once you've established setting, characters, and catalysts, it's time for change. The conflicts you set up with conventions play out in the obligatory moments.

Remember, stories are about change. Of course, we see many changes, both small and large within a story that works. But at key moments the value shifts are more pronounced. Your readers will recognize and appreciate these moments. We're confident you've felt them before, even if you didn't know what to call them. These are the obligatory moments.

A point of clarification: We've used the term "obligatory scenes" in the past, but the truth is these are *moments of change* and sometimes can be reduced to a beat or even a paragraph within a scene, so we now call them obligatory *moments*.

What kinds of moments are we talking about? *Unexpected events, revelations, and decisions.* Let's take a closer look at the types of moments that cause change in stories.

## Unexpected Events

Unexpected events that arise from characters with opposing goals naturally create responsive conflict. Even when the shadow agent is a shark or a killer storm or harsh climate, the nature of the force of antagonism opposes a luminary agent's need to survive. The shadow agent attacks, and the luminary agent reacts, and both continue in this way pursuing their goals.

The first type of unexpected event we encounter in a story is the *inciting incident*, which kicks off the primary conflict in the story.

- In *Treasure Island,* Billy Bones brings a treasure map to Jim's home at the Admiral Benbow Inn and warns him about a seafaring man with one leg.
- In *Murder on the Orient Express,* Ratchett is found murdered in his compartment aboard the train.
- In *Pride & Prejudice,* Elizabeth meets

Mr. Darcy at the Meryton Assembly ball.

Other unexpected events cause irreversible change in a *turning point progressive complication*, forcing the luminary agent to confront a dilemma. Sometimes the *resolution* is an unexpected response from the shadow agent or other agent in the arena.

- Billy Bones dies leaving his map to Jim (turning point). When Jim shares the map with Dr. Livesey and Squire Trelawney, the adults suggest they go after the treasure (resolution).
- Poirot finds a scrap of paper referring to Daisy Armstrong, which helps Poirot realize Ratchett's true identity (turning point).
- Lydia Bennet runs away with George Wickham (turning point). When Elizabeth learns of Darcy's sacrifice, she regrets her earlier treatment and decides to commit to him in marriage (resolution).

## Revelations

Revelations are *turning point progressive complications* that happen under two circumstances. New information may come from a character or the arena, or the protagonist may gain a new perspective on information they already know. Either way, they have a clearer view of their situation.

- Jim learns that Silver is a dangerous pirate who intends to kill the innocent crew members.
- Poirot realizes that the two mysterious people mentioned by the passengers can't be found on the train.
- And in a double revelation, Elizabeth and Darcy both see their relationship in a new light when she realizes her family is as ridiculous as Darcy says, and Darcy realizes he is as prideful as Elizabeth claims.

## Decisions

Decisions are climactic moments of change that happen when unexpected events and revelations give rise to a dilemma or crisis. The luminary agent exercises their agency in the arena to change themselves and their circumstances.

- Jim decides to keep the map rather than give it to pirates.
- Poirot decides justice has been done and he will tell the authorities that the murderer most likely escaped out the window.
- Elizabeth decides to reject Darcy's proposal.

Obligatory moments are the great connectors of any story. They connect the macro and micro units and combine structure and genre content. We align them with the Five Commandments of each of the major parts of a story: the beginning hook, middle build one, middle build two, and ending payoff. Each part is about 25 percent of the story and includes the inciting incident, turning point progressive complication, crisis, climax, and resolution, all influenced by the core need and value of the Four Core Framework.

We've broken down the components of the story bridge and looked at them in isolation. Now let's put them back together.

## 8

## PUTTING IT ALL TOGETHER

Here's a quick recap of what we know:

- *Conventions* are selective and enabling constraints that set up the global human value change and reader expectations in a story. They create the problem, and the means of solving it, through characters and circumstances that move the plot forward.
- *Obligatory moments* are unexpected events, revelations, or decisions that change the human value and pay off reader expectations in a story.
- *Conventions and obligatory moments* create the bridge: a sequential, incremental cause-and-effect pattern that's unique to each story

genre, delivering the experience the reader seeks.

Let's look at all of the bridge components working together in *Treasure Island*.

**What's the Genre?** The global genre is *Action*, the subgenre is *Duel* (human against human), with a *Hunted plot* (shadow agent chases the luminary agent).

## Four Core Framework

When attacked by pirates who want the treasure map he holds, Jim Hawkins needs to survive (core need), which creates change on the Death–Life spectrum (core value), evoking Excitement (core emotion) when he outwits the pirates in the *Hero at the Mercy of the Shadow Agent Scene* (core event).

## Selective Constraints: The Setting

- *Primary Locations:* Admiral Benbow Inn on the coast near Bristol, England, the open sea aboard the *Hispaniola*, and a tropical Caribbean island
- *Period:* Eighteenth century
- *Duration:* A little less than a year.

- *Levels of Conflict:* Silver and the pirates chase Jim and threaten his life because they want the map and treasure (personal conflict). The characters are susceptible to fatal tropical fevers circulating on the island (extrapersonal conflict). Jim is unsure what strategy he should adopt to defeat the pirates (inner conflict). The three forms of conflict all complicate Jim's efforts to survive.

**Enabling Constraints: Characters and Catalysts**

- *Luminary Agent:* Jim Hawkins
- *Agency-Deprived:* Jim, Dr. Livesey, Squire Trelawney, and the innocent members of the crew, which Jim calls the faithful party.
- *Shadow Agent:* Long John Silver and the other pirates
- *Speech in Praise of the Shadow Agent:* Long John Silver's recruitment speech to Dick while Jim hides in an apple barrel nearby. This speech establishes the power divide and the pirate's MacGuffin or object of desire and reason for pursuing it.

- *Deadline:* This catalyst intensifies the conflict by giving the luminary agent very little time in which to solve the primary problem. Jim and the others must defeat the pirates before they find the treasure and leave them marooned on the island.
- *Set-Piece Action Sequences:* These sequences are mini-stories of two or more scenes. The luminary agent showcases their skills and worldview to solve a smaller task as part of their overall strategy. In one sequence in the middle build, the faithful party are stuck on the island in a stockade, and the pirates have control of the ship. Jim slips out and finds the *Hispaniola* attended by two drunk pirates. He rows a small boat out to the ship, cuts it adrift, and then boards and dispatches the pirates. He then manages to stow the ship in a safe and relatively hidden location before returning to land.

## Obligatory Moments

As a reminder, obligatory moments taken together align with the structure of the Five

Commandments of Storytelling within each of the four main parts of the story (beginning hook, middle build one, middle build two, and ending payoff). This is true of any story. But the nature of these events is influenced by the genre's core need (survival) and core value (Death–Life).

*Beginning Hook*

- Attack (inciting incident): Billy Bones arrives at the Admiral Benbow Inn and warns Jim about a seafaring man with one leg.
- Sensing disorder (turning point progressive complication): Bones dies, and pirates descend on the inn searching for the map.
- Running away to reluctant engagement (crisis): Should Jim give up the map or try to keep it?
- Agreeing to fight (climax): He keeps the map, and he and his mother hide near the inn until the pirates are chased away.
- Fix-it-and-forget-it mission (resolution): Jim tells Dr. Livesey and Squire Trelawney about the map, and the three of them decide

to embark on a voyage to get the treasure.

*Middle Build One*

- A whole new world (inciting incident): Jim travels to Bristol and meets Long John Silver, a seafaring man with one leg, who will be the cook on their crew.
- Luminary agent becomes target (turning point progressive complication): Jim learns that Silver is the leader of a group of pirates masquerading as crew members on the ship. They plan to kill Jim and the faithful party of innocent crew members.
- Comply or defy? (crisis): When they reach the island and the captain allows the pirates to go ashore, should Jim stay on the ship with Dr Livesey or go ashore?
- Luminary agent responds in an unexpected way, and shadow agent attacks again (climax): Jim jumps into one of the boats going ashore. Silver tries to catch him on the island, but Jim runs.
- Point of no return (resolution): Jim

escapes from the pirates by running into the center of the island. Honest members of the crew are killed, and soon the faithful party loses control of the ship.

*Middle Build Two*

- Encounter with the unexplained (inciting incident): Jim meets Ben Gunn, a pirate marooned on the island for many years who gives him information.
- All is lost (turning point progressive complication): The faithful party seeks shelter in a stockade on shore, and when they won't give up the map, the pirates attack, killing a member of the crew and wounding others.
- How can my death be meaningful? (crisis): Should Jim take Ben Gunn's boat out to the *Hispaniola* and cut it loose or not.
- Absolute commitment (climax): Jim sets the ship adrift but then boards and dispatches the two pirates left guarding it.
- Preparations to enter the ultimate arena (resolution): Jim secures the

ship in a safe place and returns to the stockade where he's captured by the pirates.

*Ending Payoff*

- No holds barred (inciting incident): Silver convinces the pirates not to kill Jim because he now holds the map. Jim promises to speak up for Silver if he's ever caught by the British authorities.
- Death is imminent (turning point progressive complication): When the pirates follow the map, they find the treasure has already been taken. They turn on Silver and Jim.
- Do the ends justify the means? (crisis): Does Jim work with Silver to outwit the other pirates or not?
- Luminary agent at the mercy of the shadow agent (climax and core event): Jim joins Silver, and the two fight the pirates. The remaining members of the faithful party arrive, and soon they kill or chase the pirates.
- The reward (resolution): Jim and the faithful party leave the island with much of the treasure, and Silver

escapes when they stop for supplies. Jim continues to have nightmares about Silver after he returns to England.

Can you see how the conventions and obligatory moments come together to set up and pay off the reader's expectations of the core need of Survival, the core values, Life–Death, and the core emotion, Excitement?

For a deeper exploration of the Action genre, including the conventions and obligatory moments, see *Action Story: The Primal Genre* by Shawn Coyne. To find the conventions and obligatory moments for other genres, search by the genre at StoryGrid.com or check out this post with a list of the *Story Grid Editor Roundtable*'s episodes with genres noted: https://storygrid.com/editor-roundtable-episodes/.

## 9

BUILDING YOUR BRIDGE

We've explained the nature and function of conventions and obligatory moments and how they work together to create the universal patterns of story and genre that our soul's narrative receptors are wired to recognize. Now it's time to return to your story and build your own bridge.

Applying the universal patterns you've learned here, you can extrapolate the specifics of your unique Action or Crime or Love Story —or whatever genre you're writing—using your preferred story creation process.

Whatever process you use is valid. Hard core plotters may identify the conventions and obligatory moments in advance. Pure pantsers may write an exploratory draft to figure out what they want to say and then start plugging in the pieces. Many writers do a little of both. You do you, as they say! Readers don't care about your process, so long as your story includes these must-have elements. They simply want the experience you promise.

## A Final Checklist

We hope this book provides some solutions to problems that stumped you before. You'll still wrestle with things, but this time you'll have the tools to solve them.

To assess whether you've applied all the tools, ask yourself a few questions:

- Have I identified my genre and its corresponding Four Core Framework?
- Do my characters, setting, and initial circumstances implicate the opening universal human value for my genre?
- Do they create the conditions for change along my genre's universal human value spectrum?
- Do they set up a risk to the human need associated with the genre?
- Do the obligatory moments cause a change in the human value?
- Is the core event the climactic height of stakes for your

protagonist? And does it evoke the core emotion?

- Are the setting, characters, catalysts, and moments of change clear enough to communicate the setup and pay off genre expectations?

If your answer to one or more of these questions is *no*, you need to try again. But do not dismay. Every iteration of your story provides an opportunity to level up your craft.

Answering *yes* doesn't mean you're done, but it means you have met some objective targets to show you're on the right track.

At this point you have the tools you need to create a story that works and that will satisfy some readers. And while this is a great place to start, you don't have to stop here. We want to encourage you to take your craft further and express your gift unconditionally.

## 10

# CRAFTING YOUR UNIQUE BRIDGE

You've put so much work into your story, you've tried to make it more *universal,* but how do you make it *unique?*

The answer is through innovation. But how do you accomplish that?

There are many ways to innovate—a unique narrative device, offbeat style combination, or transplanting your premise to a different reality genre. But if we're talking about building your unique bridge, you need to find ways to write conventions and obligatory moments that are similar to but different from the way other writers have written them.

The first step is to study masterworks so you know what's been done in the past. Masterworks are brilliant, timeless stories at the top of a genre.

Here's what masterworks provide:

*Concrete Examples:* The abstract concepts of conventions and obligatory moments come alive when you see concrete examples in a masterwork. When our clients are confused about writing a particular obligatory event, looking at how writers they admire have done it opens up the vast array of possibilities.

*Points of Comparison:* Seeing specific conventions and obligatory moments in a variety of contexts helps you gain a deeper understanding of what the stories within your genre have in common and how your story fits or doesn't fit.

*Tips on Where and Why:* Masterworks show us *where* to place the conventions and obligatory moments in our stories, and they often teach us *why* we should use them as well.

Choosing a few masterworks isn't difficult. Find stories that are as close as possible to the one you want to write. Shawn Coyne often asks, "If you had a magic wand and could be the author of any story already published, what would it be?" That will help guide you toward your first masterwork.

Another step toward your unique story is mastering your raw materials, the stuff of your imagination.

Did you think we'd forgotten about this?

Nope. *Your individual lens, shaped by your individual experiences and knowledge, is required.*

Your raw materials must be refined, which takes self-awareness, perseverance, consideration, intention and attention—the skills of a master craftsperson. One way to refine your raw materials is to interrogate your story's premise.

- What's your point? Why are you writing *this* story? Why does it matter to you?
- What's the setting and historical context? What imbalances in power and resources lurk beneath the surface?
- Who is the luminary agent? What do they want and why?
- Who is the shadow agent? What do they want and why?
- What is the nature of the conflict between the luminary and shadow agents, including the levels of conflict?

Look at these elements from every vantage point you can think of and consider the relationships between them. Instead of running with your first idea, what other options can you think of? Consider ten to twenty alternatives by asking, *what if?*

Do the alternatives you come up with add to and support your main idea and purpose? Or do they undermine the story you want to tell?

Plumb the depths and then trust your intuition because it springs from the narrative receptors of your own soul.

# CONCLUSION

Let's return to the question all writers start with: How can we transform our initial spark of inspiration—our mind's raw materials—into a story we love and that satisfies our readers? As we've said, to do that we must turn the raw materials into a bridge that can reach our readers' narrative receptors. We choose a genre, learn its conventions and obligatory moments, and understand their meaning and function within a story. We develop an intimate relationship with story structure.

We can start anywhere, but we must complete all the steps.

We apply what we've learned by writing, writing, and writing some more. In other words, we gain understanding and then apply it over and over again, honing our craft. In this way, we'll transform what we've learned from others into skills we can own forever—and as our skills grow, we become empowered, exercising our agency.

We also seek excellent examples—those all-important masterworks. We make sure our masterworks are diverse, so we're not operating with blinders on. We study stories across many time periods and cultures, by authors of all races, ethnicities, genders, and sexualities. By studying masterworks, we test our understanding and watch principles of good writing operate in different worlds. We don't want to imitate the masters, but we can learn from them and then bring our unique perspective to new stories, improving with each draft—from the first to the fifteenth!

We always remember that the goal is a *soul-to-soul connection* that allows readers to receive and understand our unique expression.

When we share our work, we build and cross a bridge of words that connects readers across time and space.

The cool thing is, by understanding how conventions and obligatory moments work, we gain a process we can use to solve many problems that arise in our writing life. We can follow these steps:

- Identify the problem, consult resources, learn specifics, and understand the greater context.

- Gather multiple perspectives by reading masterworks within and outside our genre with our new lens.
- Practice applying what we've learned.

By embracing the craft in this way, we'll write the best story we can at this very moment.

Where should we go now that this book is done?

Let's take at least twenty minutes *today* to begin applying what we've learned to our own story. Then do it again tomorrow and the next day and the next.

## ABOUT THE AUTHORS

**KIMBERLY KESSLER** is a Story Grid Certified Editor, TEDx speaker, and one-fourth of the Story Grid Editor Roundtable Podcast. As an editor, she specializes in crafting authentic character arcs and internally driven stories. As a novelist and filmmaker, she uses humor as a means to cope with and explore trauma— ultimately, so we can find a redemptive perspective on pain. She lives in Washington state with her stand-up comedian husband and three "think they're a comedian" kids. You can connect with her directly at www.kimberkessler.com.

**LESLIE WATTS** is a Story Grid Certified Editor, writer, and podcaster based in Austin, Texas. She's been writing for as long as she can remember—from her sixth-grade magazine about cats to writing practice while drafting opinions for an appellate court judge. Leslie has co-authored *The Tipping Point by Malcolm Gladwell: A Story Grid Masterworks Analysis Guide* and *What's the Big Idea? Nonfiction Condensed*, both with Shelley Sperry. As an editor, Leslie helps fiction and nonfiction clients write epic stories that matter. She believes writers become better storytellers through study and practice and editors owe a duty of care to help writers with specific and supportive guidance. You can find her online at Writership.com.

Made in the USA
Las Vegas, NV
13 October 2023

79044382R10051